SECRET NINJA FORCE

by Julia March

Editor Rosie Peet
Designer Sam Bartlett
Senior Editor Emma Grange
Pre-production Producer Rebecca Fallowfield
Producer Louise Daly
Managing Editor Paula Regan
Design Manager Jo Connor
Publisher Julie Ferris
Art Director Lisa Lanzarini
Publishing Director Simon Beecroft

First American Edition, 2017
Published in the United States by DK Publishing
345 Hudson Street, New York, New York 10014

Page design copyright © 2017 Dorling Kindersley Limited
DK, a Division of Penguin Random House LLC

16 17 18 19 10 9 8 7 6 5 4 3 2
003–299083–Aug/17

A catalog record for this book is available from
the Library of Congress.

ISBN 978-1-4654-6196-4 (Hardback)
ISBN 978-1-4654-6195-7 (Paperback)

DK books are available at special discounts when
purchased in bulk for sales promotions, premiums,
fund-raising, or educational use. For details, contact:
DK Publishing Special Markets, 345 Hudson Street,
New York, New York 10014 SpecialSales@dk.com

Printed and bound in U.S.A.

A WORLD OF IDEAS:
SEE ALL THERE IS TO KNOW

www.dk.com
www.LEGO.com

Contents

Protectors of Ninjago® City

Master Wu is a wise teacher. He lives on a wooden fishing boat in Ninjago® Harbor. The boat is very old, just like Master Wu.

Master Wu is an expert in an ancient ninja art called Spinjitzu. He has decided to teach it to a new generation of ninja.

This group of six friends go to Ninjago High School. They are a very mixed bunch.

Poor Lloyd is not very popular, because his dad is a well-known bad guy.

Jay

Nya

Lloyd

Nya is super smart. Cole loves rock music. Kai is a chatterbox. Zane is always cracking bad jokes. Jay is a bit of a worrier.

Master Wu

Zane

Cole

Kai

Lloyd, Nya, Cole, Kai, Zane,
and Jay are not regular teens. They
are part of the Secret Ninja Force!
After school, they head to Master
Wu's boat for training sessions.

The friends must hide their true
identities. It's an important part
of being a ninja. Don't give away
their secret!

Ninja fact files

Each ninja has different talents.
Master Wu must teach them to
combine their talents. Then, they
will be an unstoppable team.

LLOYD

Title: The Green Ninja

Talent: Being a great
team leader

NYA

Title: The Gray Ninja

Talents: Confident and
adaptable to new
situations

KAI

Title: The Red Ninja

Talents: Being brave—and
chatty!

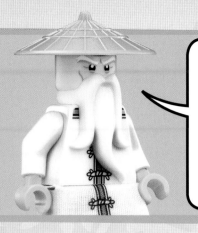

I chose my ninja carefully. Each brings something different to the team.

COLE

Title: The Black Ninja

Talent: Always cool and calm

JAY

Title: The Blue Ninja

Talent: Always eager to help

ZANE

Title: The White Ninja

Talent: Stays focused

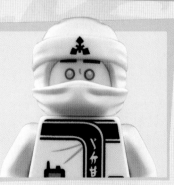

Meet the ninja

Lloyd often gets mean comments from his classmates. That's because his dad is Lord Garmadon, the worst villain in Ninjago® City. It's really unfair, because Lloyd doesn't even get along with his dad. In fact, as the leader of the Secret Ninja Force, he has to fight him!

As the Green Ninja, Lloyd wears green armor. His favorite weapon is a sword.

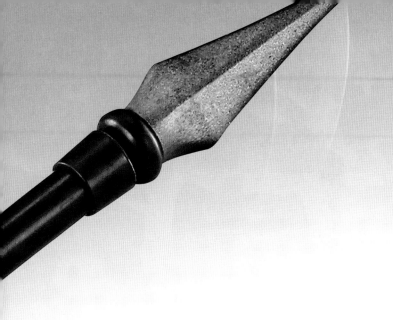

Nya is a great all-rounder. She's a fast learner. She has awesome fighting skills. She's great at solving problems, too. She can be a little competitive, especially with her brother Kai!

Nya is the Gray Ninja. Her favorite weapon is a spear.

Cole is as cool as a cucumber. He never gets upset. Well, almost never. He might complain a little if someone asks him to turn his rock music down!

Cole likes to look cool. He often can't resist snapping a selfie or two.

Cole is the Black Ninja. His favorite weapon is a hammer.

Kai is Nya's brother.
Like her, he is bold and
fearless. Unlike her, he
doesn't think before
he acts. Kai's fiery
nature gets him into
trouble all the time.
Luckily, he can usually
talk his way out of it again.

Kai is the Red Ninja. His favorite
weapons are twin katana swords.

Jay is a nervous ninja. He worries about being good enough, even when his friends tell him he is doing fine. Despite his nerves, Jay is a great ninja and a loyal friend.

Jay has a crush on his teammate, Nya. He admires her confidence.

Jay is the Blue Ninja. His favorite weapon is a nunchuck.

Zane is a nindroid, which is a type of robot. Because of this, he finds it hard to understand emotions. But being a robot means he can stay calm and focused in battle. His fellow ninja think his robot skills are awesome!

Zane is the White Ninja. His favorite weapon is a bow and arrow.

Cole is strong enough to climb the tallest mast

Traditional red dragon symbol

Master Wu's living quarters are at the back

Destiny's Bounty

Master Wu's boat is called Destiny's Bounty. This is where Master Wu eats, sleeps, drinks tea, meditates, and plays his flute. It's also the place where he trains the ninja.

Sails can be rolled up when the boat is docked

Kai practices leaping with his katanas

Dragon figures to intimidate enemies

No one quite knows what's below deck!

Ninjago® City in peril

Evil Lord Garmadon has attacked Ninjago® City countless times. Now he plans to take over the city.

Inside his volcano hideout, Garmadon questions his generals. He is very displeased with their failure to take over Ninjago City.

Garmadon is happier with his scientists. They have built some great new mechs and gadgets. He rubs his four hands together with glee.

He's here! Lord Garmadon is in Ninjago City, with a Shark Army!

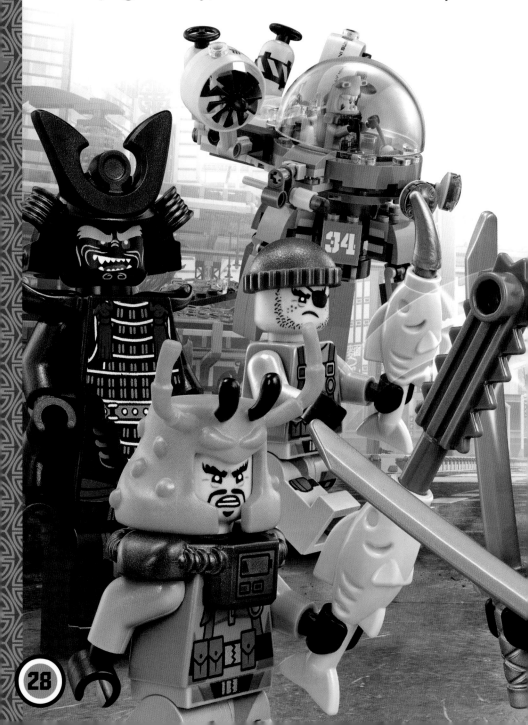

Citizens flee as Shark Soldiers fill the streets. They carry stingers, fish forks, and other weapons. They drive fishy vehicles, too.

The ninja defeat the Shark Army and save the citizens, but it's hard work. When the battle is over, the city is a wreck.

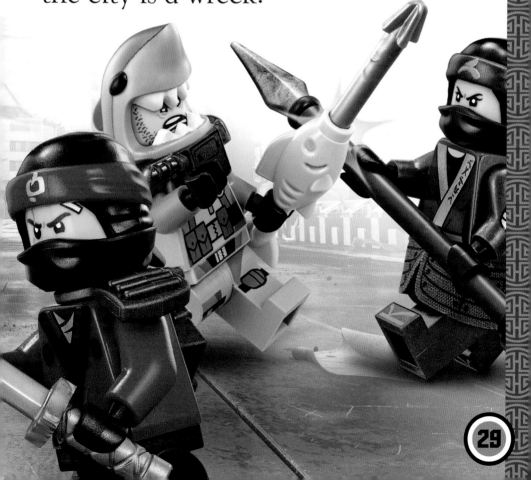

Citizen's report

Everyone is happy when the ninja crush Garmadon. They are not so happy with the mess! Here's what Ninjago® City's citizens are saying about the heroes.

That Gray Ninja trampled my Taco Tuk Tuk in her mech. Grrr!

The Red Ninja put me in a safe place—a sewer hole. Yuk!

Blue Ninja? Blew up my house, more like!

My car is ruined, but I'm alive! Thanks, Green Ninja!

Hey, White Ninja! How about helping me rebuild my house?

the Secret Ninja Squad save it from Garmadon.

Ninja gear

The ninja know that Garmadon will be back. They believe they can beat him again if they build even better mechs. Master Wu does not agree. He tells the ninja to work on their Spinjitzu skills. Then they might defeat Garmadon for good.

This is not what the ninja want to hear. They love their mechs!

Zane's Ice Tank

Cole's Quake Mech

Jay's Electric Jaybird Mech

Kai's Fireman Mech

Lloyd's Dragon Mech

Nya's Waterbug Mech

Mech design

Lloyd designs all the ninja mechs. He plans them out carefully on graph paper before he starts to build. Here is the design for Kai's Fireman Mech.

Transparent cockpit

Triple-nozzle flame gun

Fire transfer pipe

Large feet for stability

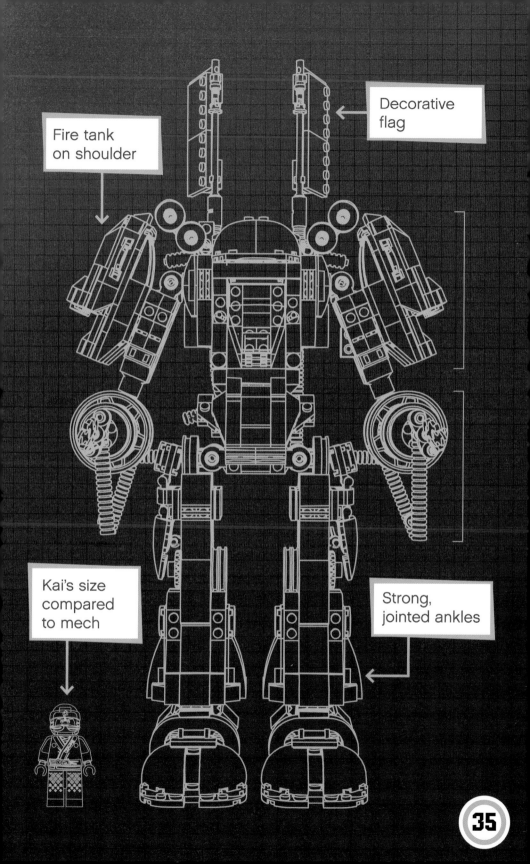

Fire tank
on shoulder

Decorative
flag

Kai's size
compared
to mech

Strong,
jointed ankles

Master Wu decides to trust Lloyd
with a secret. He shows Lloyd where
he has hidden something awesome.
It's the Ultimate Weapon! Wu tells
Lloyd not to try to use it himself.
Later, Lloyd sneaks back
and takes the weapon.

Lloyd threatens Garmadon
with the Ultimate Weapon,
but Garmadon grabs it from him.
Ninjago City is soon in ruins.

Master Wu's warnings

Lloyd thought that the Ultimate Weapon was the answer to all their problems. Master Wu reminds the team that being a true ninja takes more than cool gadgets.

> Do not rely only on fancy mechs and weapons. What will you do if they are not there?

> A true ninja relies on traditional ninja skills instead.

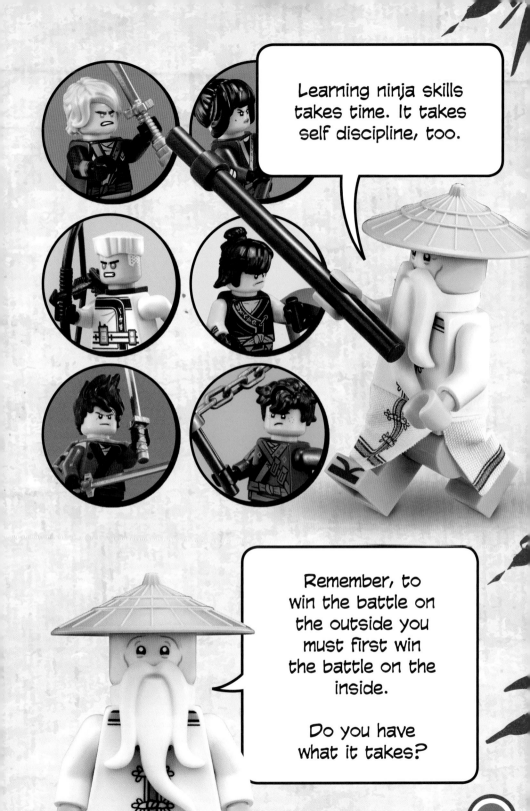

True ninja

Oh no! The ninja are lost in a scary jungle. They have taken Garmadon prisoner, and they must get him home before he escapes.

The ninja must remember the skills Wu has taught them. Skills such as moving silently and sensing danger in the air. Slowly, they practice. Slowly, they become true ninja.

The ninja have learned to use their instincts. Now they can learn the art of Spinjitzu.

With Spinjitzu, a ninja can create a tornado of power. A team of ninja working together could create a tornado powerful enough to rebuild a whole city.

The ninja come together. They are ready to save Ninjago® City!

Quiz

1. Why is Lloyd unpopular at school?

2. What ancient ninja art does Master Wu teach?

3. What kind of weapon does Nya use?

4. What is the name of Master Wu's fishing boat?

5. Why is Garmadon pleased with his scientists?

6. Which ninja uses a bow and arrow?

7. What is the name of Garmadon's army?

8. True or false: Master Wu tells Lloyd to use the Ultimate Weapon.

Answers on page 48

Glossary

Competitive
Wanting to win at everything

Instincts
Natural abilities or senses that you are born with

Katanas
Swords with long, thin, curved blades

Potential
Something that has not happened
yet, but might happen in
the future

Ultimate
Greatest, most extreme

Guide for Parents

This book is part of an exciting four-level reading series for children, developing the habit of reading widely for both pleasure and information. These chapter books have a compelling main narrative to suit your child's reading ability. Each book is designed to develop your child's reading skills, fluency, grammar awareness, and comprehension in order to build confidence and engagement when reading.

Ready for a *Level 2* book

YOUR CHILD SHOULD

- be familiar with using beginning letter sounds and context clues to figure out unfamiliar words.
- be aware of the need for a slight pause at commas and a longer one at periods.
- alter his/her expression for questions and exclamations.

A VALUABLE AND SHARED READING EXPERIENCE

For many children, reading requires much effort, but adult participation can make this both fun and easier. So here are a few tips on how to use this book with your child.

TIP 1 **Check out the contents together before your child begins:**

- read the text about the book on the back cover.
- flip through the book and stop to chat about the contents page together to heighten your child's interest and expectation.
- make use of unfamiliar or difficult words on the page in a brief discussion.
- chat about the nonfiction reading features used in the book, such as headings, captions, lists, or charts.

TIP 2 Support your child as he/she reads the story pages:

- give the book to your child to read and turn the pages.

- where necessary, encourage your child to break a word into syllables, sound out each one, and then flow the syllables together. Ask him/her to reread the sentence to check the meaning.

- when there's a question mark or an exclamation mark, encourage your child to vary his/her voice as he/she reads the sentence. Demonstrate how to do this if it is helpful.

TIP 3 Chat at the end of each page:

- ask questions about the text and the meaning of the words used. These help to develop comprehension skills and awareness of the language used.

A FEW ADDITIONAL TIPS

- Always encourage your child to try reading difficult words by themselves. Praise any self-corrections, for example, "I like the way you sounded out that word and then changed the way you said it, to make sense."

- Try to read together everyday. Reading little and often is best. These books are divided into manageable chapters for one reading session. However, after 10 minutes, only keep going if your child wants to read on.

- Read other books of different types to your child just for enjoyment and information.

Index

Answers to the quiz on page 44:
1. His dad is Lord Garmadon 2. Spinjitzu 3. A spear 4. Destiny's Bounty 5. They have built him some new mechs and gadgets 6. Zane 7. The Shark Army 8. False—he tells him not to use it.